Mozart

Flute Concertos

edited by Trevor Wye
piano arrangements by Robert Scott

Concerto No. 1 in G   K.313

NOVELLO

Order No: NOV 120577

PREFACE

Both Mozart's flute concertos, K.313 and 314, and the Andante in C for flute, K.315, were written in Mannheim in 1778 in order to fulfil a commission. When he completed the Concerto in G, Mozart found time running short, so he transcribed and tranposed his earlier Oboe Concerto in C to make the second Flute Concerto.

The only surviving autograph scores are of the Andante and the oboe solo part of the Oboe Concerto, though the latter copy is not regarded as authentic. It is possible that the Andante may have been written as an easier alternative to the second movement of K.314.

Tuttis have been omitted from this edition; editorial additions are marked in dotted lines, deleted slurs, or are in brackets, and interpretations of ornaments are placed above the stave. Unless otherwise indicated, the earliest known sources have been adhered to; the flute parts can therefore be considered 'urtext'.

In most, if not all present day editions, the piano parts are a reduction of the original orchestral score and are generally unplayable by all but the most advanced pianists. Since the concertos are often performed with piano, we have approached the problem of orchestral reduction in the way Mozart might have done — by writing for the piano in its own right and not as a substitute for the chamber orchestra. We have modelled the piano part on Mozart's piano and violin sonata writing and inessential material has been omitted. However, the original notation has been preserved where possible, including the bowing of the string parts.

Ornaments   C. P. E. Bach wrote that nobody ever doubted ornaments were necessary. Because there were always so many of them, they served to link notes together, to enliven notes and sometimes to emphasise or draw attention to them. However, Mozart wrote these concertos during a change in ornamental style, so it is especially difficult to know exactly how these ornaments should be played. In this edition the performer can see the earliest written sources and judge for himself. On the other hand, those with little specialist knowledge may care to follow the suggestion placed in brackets, or above the stave, which are based on present-day informed opinion★. Some of these suggestions may not fall easily on ears accustomed to other, older interpretations. Recent interest in performances using eighteenth-century instruments has drawn attention to unstylish, nineteenth-century versions to which the public has become accustomed.

Other editorial markings   Some nuances have been included in brackets. Slurs which might well have been used in Mozart's time have been suggested by dotted lines. As a general guide, slurred pairs of notes throughout these works should be played with the second note softer and slightly shorter.

Mozart, or his copyist, wrote in many slurs. Those who wish to play with fewer 'bumps' and with long, vocal phrases as in the nineteenth century, should omit the slurs with a line through them indicated thus: ⌐╫

★E. and P. Badura-Skoda: Interpreting Mozart on the Keyboard (Barrie & Rockcliffe)
★Franz Vester: On the Performance of Mozart's Flute Music (N.F.A.)
★B. B. Mather and D. Lasocki: The Classical Woodwind Cadenza (McGinnis & Marz)
★J. J. Quantz: 'Versuch' (1752)
★Grove: Dictionary of Music and Musicians (Macmillan)

PERFORMING SUGGESTIONS

The two ornaments found in these works are *appoggiaturas* and *trills*. It is just as important to understand the *style* of playing them as it is to determine the *rhythm*. The suggested rhythm has been placed either in brackets or above the stave.

Concerto No. 1 in G

Accented appoggiaturas　These were originally accented passing notes. Their value is deducted from the following note.

First movement. Bars 32, 36, 38 and 39: 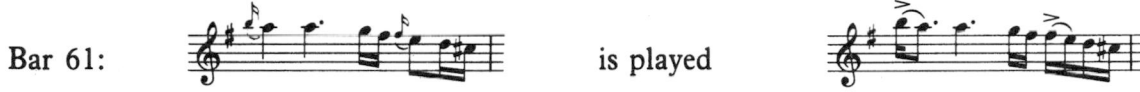 is played though some prefer the first note to be played shorter: . If the latter interpretation is adopted, it must be used consistently throughout the movement.

Bar 61: 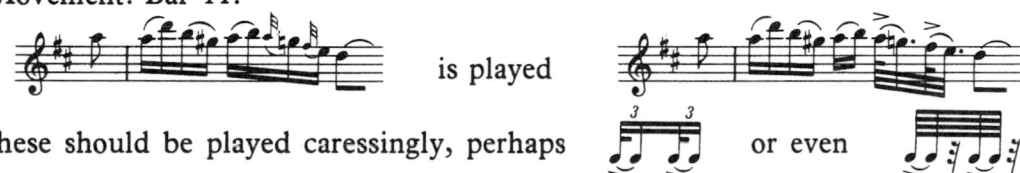 is played

The first appoggiatura is accented in each case *and the second note played softer*.

Second Movement. Bar 11:  is played

though these should be played caressingly, perhaps or even

because of their melodic expressiveness. The style of playing an accented first note and softer second note *are just as important as the rhythm*.

Unaccented appoggiaturas
First Movement. Bar 46:  is played

Rising, instead of falling, appoggiaturas, are almost always played unaccented and short. According to Leopold Mozart, they are to be played 'as rapidly as possible'. The accent falls on the principal note. They are played less fast in slow movements.

The compound appoggiaturas found in bars 72 and 220 of the third movement should be played quickly and caressingly, the first note of which should be *on* the beat.

Trills　All trills begin on the upper note except sometimes; the exceptions are shown in the flute part either by the omission of an auxiliary note, or by the inclusion of the *lower* auxiliary. The auxiliary note, when present, is played *on* the beat.

　At the end of trills turns have sometimes been suggested; where there are none marked, none should be played.

Cadenzas   These generally appear toward the end of the movement, and are intended to surprise and delight the audience and to keep them in suspense with the six-four chord. Contrary to present-day popular belief, it was not usual to employ thematic material from the concerto in a cadenza. The player only used thematic material when his imagination had run dry. Nevertheless, it *could* be used, or the cadenza might be built simply of scales and arpeggios with a passing reference to a theme or two. The music must maintain the suspense after the six-four chord, until the arrival of the inevitable dominant seventh chord and its resolution. Because a flute player must breathe and because he can only play one note at a time, flute cadenzas were often short and limited to only a few breaths.

Write your own. Better still, write down several ideas and when stuck, start another. Don't wander into odd keys. Try to sound Mozartian. Does your cadenza contain surprise? Does it suit the movement? Is it interesting? Does it flow smoothly? Does it show off your ability as a player?

Combine your ideas and you will have made a start. Try to play all cadenzas spontaneously, as if you are making them up as you go along. The six-four chord at the beginning of the cadenza is not resolved. If you are playing the concertos with piano, the pianist might put in the dominant seventh halfway or two thirds of the way through the trill, depending on the time signature, as indicated in this edition.

It is well to remember that unless the concerto movement has been brilliantly played, you have nothing to cadenza about—in which case a short one is preferable!

TREVOR WYE, 1983

CONCERTO No.1 IN G, K.313

Edited by Trevor Wye
Piano arrangement by Robert Scott

W. A. MOZART

1

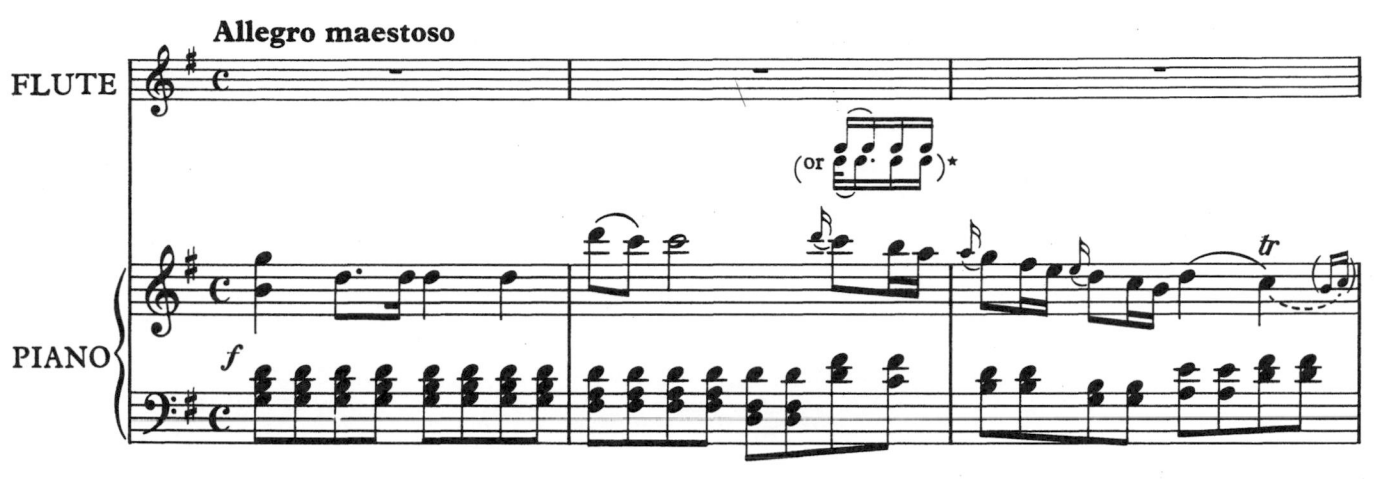

*See Preface

2

Ped.

* See Preface

* See Preface

9

*An F♯ appears here in some editions. It makes musical sense but until an autograph is found, doubts will remain.

14

16

(cresc.)

cresc.

206

(f)

f

209

(See Preface)

213

(f)

f

216

2

Adagio non troppo

18

* See Preface

20

24

(See Preface)

54

57

59

61

25

3

Rondo. Tempo di Menuetto

28

140

144

148

152

(simile)   (cresc.)   157

(f)   (See Preface)   (p)   162

(cresc.)   167

(f)   173

MUSIC FOR FLUTE

TUTORS

WYE, Trevor
A BEGINNER'S BOOK FOR THE FLUTE
Part 1 (Cassette also available)
Part 2

A PRACTICE BOOK FOR THE FLUTE:
VOLUME 1 Tone (Cassette also available)
VOLUME 2 Technique
VOLUME 3 Articulation
VOLUME 4 Intonation and vibrato
VOLUME 5 Breathing and scales
VOLUME 6 Advanced Practice
PROPER FLUTE PLAYING

SOLO

ALBUM
ed Trevor Wye
MUSIC FOR SOLO FLUTE
This attractive collection draws together under one cover 11 major works representing the fundamental solo flute repertoire, edited in a clear and practical form.

trans Gordon Saunders
EIGHT TRADITIONAL JAPANESE PIECES
Gordon Saunders has selected and transcribed these pieces for tenor recorder solo or flute from the traditional folk music of Japan.

FLUTE AND PIANO

ALBUMS
arr Barrie Carson Turner
CHRISTMAS FUN BOOK
CLASSICAL POPS FUN BOOK
ITALIAN OPERA FUN BOOK
MOZART FUN BOOK
POP CANTATA FUN BOOK
POPULAR CLASSICS FUN BOOK
RAGTIME FUN BOOK
TV THEME FUN BOOK

arr Trevor Wye
A VERY EASY BAROQUE ALBUM, Vols. 1 & 2
A VERY EASY CLASSICAL ALBUM
A VERY EASY ROMANTIC ALBUM
A VERY EASY 20TH CENTURY ALBUM
A FIRST LATIN-AMERICAN FLUTE ALBUM
A SECOND LATIN-AMERICAN FLUTE ALBUM

BENNETT, Richard Rodney
SUMMER MUSIC

COUPERIN, François
arr Trevor Wye
A COUPERIN ALBUM

ELGAR, Edward
arr Trevor Wye
AN ELGAR FLUTE ALBUM

FAURE, Gabriel
arr Trevor Wye
A FAURE ALBUM

FRASER, Shena
SONATINA

GALWAY, James
THE MAGIC FLUTE OF JAMES GALWAY
SHOWPIECES

HARRIS, Paul
CLOWNS

HURD, Michael
SONATINA

McCABE, John
PORTRAITS

RAMEAU, Jean Philippe
arr Trevor Wye
A RAMEAU ALBUM

RAVEL, Maurice
arr Trevor Wye
A RAVEL ALBUM

REEMAN, John
SIX FOR ONE

SATIE, Erik
arr Trevor Wye
A SATIE FLUTE ALBUM

SCHUBERT, Franz
arr Trevor Wye
THEME AND VARIATIONS D.935 No.3

SCHUMANN, Robert
arr Trevor Wye
A SCHUMANN ALBUM

SCHURMANN, Gerard
SONATINA

VIVALDI, Antonio
arr Trevor Wye
A VIVALDI ALBUM